MID-ATLANTIC WETLANDS
A Disappearing Natural Treasure

by

Ralph W. Tiner, Jr.

U.S. Fish and Wildlife Service
Fish and Wildlife Enhancement
National Wetlands Inventory Project
One Gateway Center, Suite 700
Newton Corner, Ma 02158

June 1987

COOPERATIVE PUBLICATION:

U.S. Fish and Wildlife Service
Region Five
One Gateway Center
Newton Corner, MA 02158

U.S. Environmental Protection Agency
Region Three
841 Chestnut Building
Philadelphia, PA 19107

TABLE OF CONTENTS

Bill Zinni

Copies of this booklet can be obtained from:

U.S. Environmental Protection Agency
Region III
Office of Public Affairs
(3PA00)
841 Chestnut Building
Philadelphia, PA 19107

or

U.S. Fish and Wildlife Service
Region 5
Fish and Wildlife Enhancement (NWI)
One Gateway Center
Newton Corner, MA 02158

Cover Photo by George Fenwick

Title Page Photo by Ralph Tiner

Back Cover Photo Credits: Larry Ditto (a), Pat Hagan (b); ©Mary Martin (c); Paul Wiegman (d); Dave Menke (e), USFWS (f), Ron W. Lowe (g); Donna Dewhurst (h), USFWS (i).

PREFACE

This booklet provides the general public with the most up-to-date information on the status and recent trends in wetlands of five states in the Mid-Atlantic region: Delaware, Maryland, Pennsylvania, Virginia, and West Virginia. Pertinent background information on wetland types and values is also presented along with some recommendations to improve the future for wetlands. This booklet is based on a recently completed U.S. Fish and Wildlife Service—U.S. Environmental Protection Agency study of wetland changes in this five-state region. This study was designed to answer questions such as: (1) How much wetland exists in the region?, (2) Where are wetlands most abundant?, (3) What wetland types are most common? (4) How have wetlands changed between the mid-1950's and late 1970's?, (5) What wetlands are most threatened?, and (6) What are the major causes of wetland changes? We hope that this booklet will provide you with the answers to these questions, give you a better understanding of wetlands, and spark an interest in the conservation of these valuable natural resources.

Ralph Tiner

INTRODUCTION

The collection of wet environments occurring on the landscape in the Mid-Atlantic region and elsewhere are called "*wetlands.*" They include tidal marshes and mudflats along the coast and freshwater marshes and swamps, bottomland hardwood forests, wet meadows, ponds, and bogs further inland.

In the past, wetlands were generally viewed as wastelands—places infested with mosquitoes, biting flies and poisonous snakes—and having little real or economic value. Largely because of this negative view, wetlands were regarded as potential sites for development or as convenient sites for waste disposal. In agricultural areas, many wetlands were drained, cleared, and put into crop production, while in urban areas, other wetlands were filled for houses, industrial facilities, office buildings and sanitary landfills. Consequently, today, less than half of America's original wetlands remain.

During the past thirty years, our knowledge about wetlands and their natural values has greatly increased. We now know that wetlands are important natural resources that provide numerous benefits to our society. First, wetlands are the vital habitats for many plants and animals. In fact, the majority of our threatened and endangered plant species and many endangered animals depend on wetlands for survival. Wetlands also provide more direct values to people in many ways, such as improving water quality, reducing flood and storm damages, minimizing erosion of upland, and supporting tourism and the hunting and fishing industries. Because wetlands are important to people, the federal government is regulating various uses of wetlands, especially the deposition of fill in wetlands. Most Mid-Atlantic states have enacted laws to regulate specific uses of certain types of wetlands. Despite these controls, wetlands, like other natural areas, remain under increasing pressure for development as our population increases.

Phil Norton

Bittern chicks.

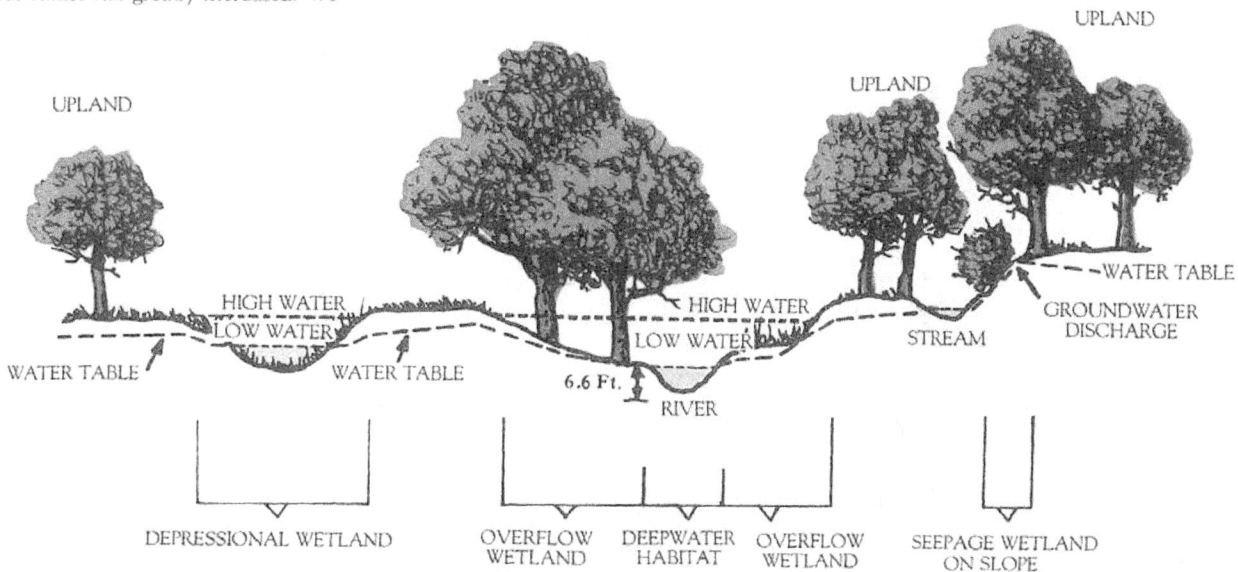

Schematic diagram showing wetlands, deepwater habitats, and uplands on the landscape. Note differences in wetlands due to hydrology and topographic position.

1

WETLAND TYPES

Just what are wetlands, you might ask? Wetlands are largely semi-aquatic lands that are flooded for varying periods of time during the growing season. When not flooded, wetland soils are often saturated near the land surface. Wetlands include areas commonly called marshes, swamps, and bogs as well as the shallow water zones of rivers, lakes, and ponds. The presence of water in these areas creates environmental conditions that affect the types of soils that develop and the types of plants and animals living there. In general, wetlands are defined by the predominance of "hydrophytes" (plants adapted for life in wet soils) and the presence of "hydric soils" (saturated or periodically flooded soils).

A variety of wetland types exist throughout the Mid-Atlantic region due to differences in climate, soil, hydrology, salinity, vegetation, and other factors. Two general types of wetlands are recognized: (1) *coastal wetlands* and (2) *inland wetlands*. Coastal wetlands consist mainly of tidal marshes and mudflats that are periodically flooded by salt or brackish water. As their name suggests, coastal wetlands are found in the Coastal Zone along tidal rivers and saltwater embayments. By contrast, inland wetlands are freshwater marshes, swamps, and bogs that are largely non-tidal (not affected by ocean-driven tides). They usually occur on floodplains along rivers and streams, along the margins of lakes and ponds, and in isolated depressions in the upland. Yet, some freshwater wetlands occur in the freshwater portions of tidal coastal rivers, such as the Potomac, Nanticoke, and Delaware rivers.

Wetlands are further characterized by their dominant vegetation as: (1) emergent wetlands (commonly called marshes and wet meadows) dominated by grasses, sedges, and other herbaceous (non-woody) plants, (2) shrub wetlands (including shrub swamps and bogs) represented by low to medium-height (less than 20 feet tall) woody plants, and (3) forested wetlands (largely wooded swamps and bottomland hardwood forests) dominated by trees (greater than 20 feet tall).

John Organ

Leatherleaf shrub bog in Pennsylvania's Pocono region.

Ralph Tiner

Many inland wetlands are mosaics of emergent, shrub, and forested wetland communities.

Ralph Tiner

Glasswort, a common salt-loving plant, occupies shallow depressions called pannes in saline coastal marshes.

2

Coastal Wetlands

Coastal marshes (also called estuarine emergent wetlands) are the dominant type of coastal wetlands. They are largely grasslands flooded by salt or brackish tidal water. Salt-tolerant grasses, including smooth cordgrass, salt hay grass, giant cordgrass, and switchgrass, generally dominate these wetlands. Other herbaceous plants, such as black needlerush, three-squares, narrow-leaved cattail, and rose mallow, may also be abundant, especially in brackish water areas. Coastal marshes can be divided into two zones based on elevation and flooding frequency: (1) low marsh—flooded at least once a day and (2) high marsh—flooded less than daily. Most of the coastal marshes in the five-state Mid-Atlantic region are high marshes associated with Chesapeake and Delaware Bays and their tributaries. Other coastal wetlands are represented by non-vegetated tidal flats and by shrub wetlands dominated by high-tide bush and groundsel tree.

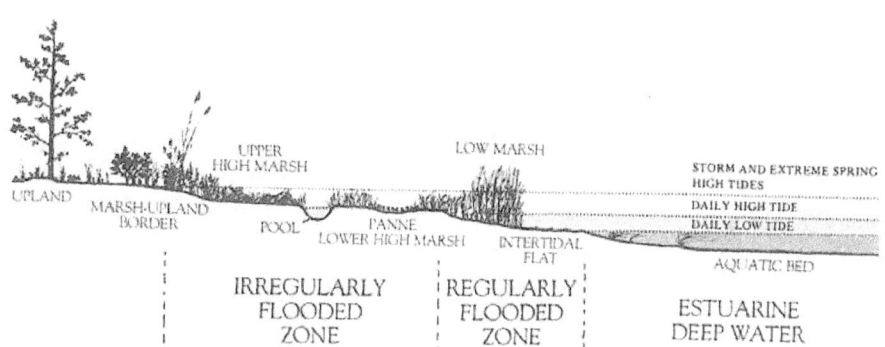

Hydrology of coastal wetlands showing different zones of flooding. The regularly flooded zone is flooded at least once daily by the tides, while the irregularly flooded zone is flooded less often.

Ralph Tiner

Salt marsh on the Eastern Shore of Virginia.

Inland Wetlands

The Mid-Atlantic region's inland wetlands are mostly non-tidal (above tidal influence). Three types are most common: (1) emergent wetlands, (2) shrub wetlands, and (3) forested wetlands. Forested wetlands are, by far, the most common type. Red maple, silver maple, black gum, willow oak, green ash, pin oak, and sweet gum are among the common trees in forested wetlands. Bald cypress is most abundant in southeastern Virginia, but also common in eastern Maryland. Common shrubs include buttonbush, swamp rose, alders, willows, and silky dogwood. Meadowsweet and leatherleaf are more typical of shrub swamps at higher elevations in the Appalachian Highlands of Pennsylvania, West Virginia, and western Maryland. Emergent wetlands are dominated by a number of herbaceous plants including broad-leaved cattail, bluejoint grass, reed canary grass, soft rush, wool grass, sedges, smartweeds, and certain asters and goldenrods.

Ralph Tiner

Bottomland hardwood forested wetlands are common along rivers throughout the region.

VALUES OF WETLANDS

Wetlands in the Mid-Atlantic region are important natural resources not only to local residents, but also to others living outside of the area who consume or utilize products produced there. At the center of the region lies Chesapeake Bay—the nation's largest estuary and a national treasure. Wetlands are vital to the well-being of the Bay and its living resources.

In their natural condition, wetlands provide many benefits including: (1) fish and wildlife habitat, (2) aquatic productivity, (3) water quality improvement, (4) flood damage protection, (5) erosion control, (6) natural products for human use, and (7) opportunities for recreation and aesthetic appreciation. Each wetland works in combination with other wetlands as part of a complex, integrated system that delivers these benefits and others to society. An assessment of the value of a particular wetland must take this critical interrelationship into account.

Fish and Wildlife Habitat

Wetlands are required by many types of animals and plants for survival. For many, like the wood duck and muskrat or cattail and swamp rose, wetlands are their primary homes or habitats—the only places they can live. For other animals, such as striped bass, the endangered peregrine falcon, or white-tailed deer, wetlands provide food, water, or cover that are important to their well-being, but wetlands are not their primary residences. It is interesting to note that the majority of rare and endangered plants in many states depend on wetlands for survival.

Coastal wetlands are particularly important habitats for estuarine and marine fishes and shellfish, various waterfowl, shorebirds and wading birds, and several mammals. Most commercial and game fishes use coastal marshes and estuaries as nursery or spawning grounds. Menhaden, bluefish, flounder, sea trout, spot, mullet, croaker, and striped bass are among the more familiar fishes that depend on coastal

wetlands. In fact, Chesapeake Bay is the major spawning and nursery grounds for striped bass on the East Coast. Blue crabs, the prized shellfish of the Bay, also depend on coastal marshes, as do other shellfish such as oysters, clams, and shrimp.

Inland wetlands are also valuable fish and wildlife habitats. Most freshwater fishes feed in wetlands or upon wetland-produced food and use wetlands as nursery grounds. Interestingly enough, almost all important recreational fishes spawn in the aquatic portions of wetlands. A variety of

birdlife is also associated with inland wetlands. Ducks, geese, redwinged blackbirds, and a large number of songbirds feed, nest and raise their young in these wetlands. Muskrat and beaver are the most familiar wetland mammals. White-tailed deer (a traditional upland game mammal) use wetlands for food and shelter, especially evergreen forested wetlands in winter. The mighty black bear finds refuge and food in forested and shrub swamps of the Pocono region of Pennsylvania and other areas.

©Mary Martin

Male wood duck.

Paul Wiegman

Spreading globe-flower—a rare wetland plant.

USFWS

Many upland animals come to wetlands for water.

4

Aquatic Productivity

Wetlands are among the most productive natural ecosystems in the world and certain types of wetlands may be the highest, rivaling our best cornfields. Wetlands can be regarded as the farmlands of the aquatic environment since great volumes of food (plant material) are produced by them annually. Although direct grazing of most wetland plants is generally limited, their major food value comes from dead leaves and stems that breakdown in the water to form small particles of organic material called "*detritus*". This enriched detritus serves as the principal food for many small aquatic invertebrates and forage fishes that are food for larger predatory fishes, such as bluefish and striped bass. These larger fishes are, in turn, consumed by people. Thus, wetlands provide an important source of food for people as well as for aquatic animals.

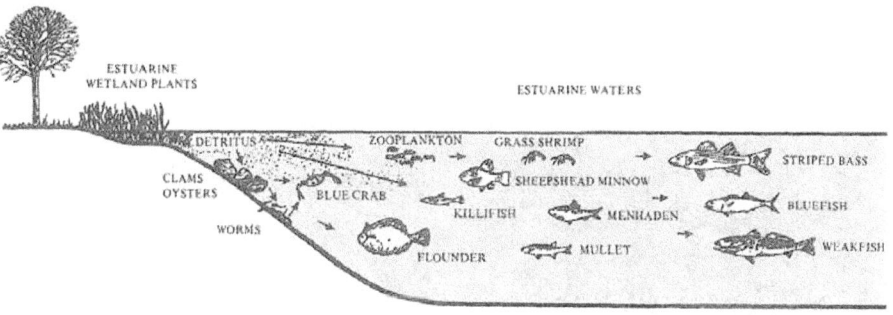

Mid-Atlantic coastal marshes annually produce over a million tons of organic material (detritus) that supports fish and shellfish important to people.

Muskrat and its lodge in a cattail marsh.

Water Quality Improvement

One of the most important values of wetlands is their ability to help maintain good water quality in our nation's rivers and other waterbodies and to improve degraded waters. Wetlands do this in several ways: (1) removing and retaining nutrients, (2) processing chemical and organic wastes, and (3) reducing sediment loads to receiving waters. Wetlands are particularly good water filters. Due to their position between upland and deep water, wetlands can both intercept surface-water runoff from land before it reaches open water and help filter nutrients, wastes, and sediment from flooding waters. This function is important in both urban and agricultural areas. The future of Chesapeake Bay depends on restoring good water quality, and protecting wetlands within the Bay's watershed are vital to this effort. Clean waters are important to people as well as to aquatic and other wildlife.

Flood Damage Protection

Wetlands have often been referred to as natural sponges that absorb flooding waters, yet they actually function more like natural tubs, storing flood waters that overflow riverbanks or surface water that collects in isolated depressions. By temporarily storing flood waters, wetlands help protect adjacent and downstream property owners from flood damage. Trees and other wetland plants help slow the speed of flood waters. This action combined with water storage allows wetlands to lower flood heights and reduce the water's erosive potential. Wetlands in and upstream of urban areas are especially valuable for flood protection, since urban development increases the rate and volume of surface-water runoff, thereby increasing the risk of flood damage. In agricultural areas, wetlands help to reduce the likelihood of flood damage to crops.

Kelly Drake

Wetlands are valuable flood storage areas; wetland destruction accelerates flood damages in urban areas.

USFWS

Highbush blueberry.

Erosion Control

Wetlands are often located between rivers and high ground and are, therefore, in a good position to buffer the land against erosion. Wetland plants are most important in this regard, since they increase the durability of the sediment through binding soil with their roots, dampen wave action by friction, and reduce current velocity through friction. The states of Delaware and Maryland are now recommending the planting of wetland vegetation to control shoreline erosion in coastal environments.

Natural Products

A wealth of natural products are produced by wetlands. Products that are available for human use include timber, fish and shell fish, wildlife, blueberries and peat moss.

Chesapeake Bay is the largest producer of blue crabs in the world and the largest single source of oysters in this country. Wetland grasses are hayed in many places for winter livestock feed and during the spring and summer, livestock graze in many freshwater marshes. In certain areas like the Poconos and western Maryland, wetlands are being mined for peat moss which is used for horticultural purposes. Harvest of peat moss requires excavation of natural wetlands which unfortunately eliminates most of the wetland's values, especially as wildlife habitat.

Recreation and Aesthetics

Many recreational activities take place in and around wetlands. Waterfowl hunting, fishing and crabbing are popular sports. Other recreation is largely non-

consumptive and involves activities like hiking, nature observation and photography, swimming, boating, and ice skating. Many people simply enjoy the beauty and sounds of nature and spend their leisure time walking or boating in or near wetlands observing plant and animal life. Through the centuries, wetlands have also captured the attention of artists who have painted wetland scenes or have written about wetlands. Thus, wetlands are without question an important part of the natural heritage of America—one of our most valuable natural treasures.

Dave Menke

a   DNREC

b   DNREC

A fringe of marsh grasses as narrow as eight feet can reduce wave energy by over 50 percent (a—during planting; b—one year later).

Wetlands offer opportunities for environmental education.

CURRENT STATUS AND RECENT TRENDS IN WETLANDS

The most recent information on the current status and recent trends in wetlands for the five Mid-Atlantic states comes from a joint U.S. Fish and Wildlife Service—U.S. Environmental Protection Agency study. Using a statistical sampling design, researchers determined wetland changes between the mid-1950's and late 1970's for this region. Four-square mile sample plots were randomly selected within each state and evaluated for change through photo interpretation techniques. By comparing aerial photos from two time periods for each plot, the extent of wetland present at both times and corresponding wetland changes (losses and gains) were identified. From this information, current wetland acreage and recent trends were estimated. The following two subsections summarize the study's findings on the current status of wetlands in each state and in the Chesapeake Bay watershed and on their recent changes.

Bill Zinni

a

Coastal Plain swamp.

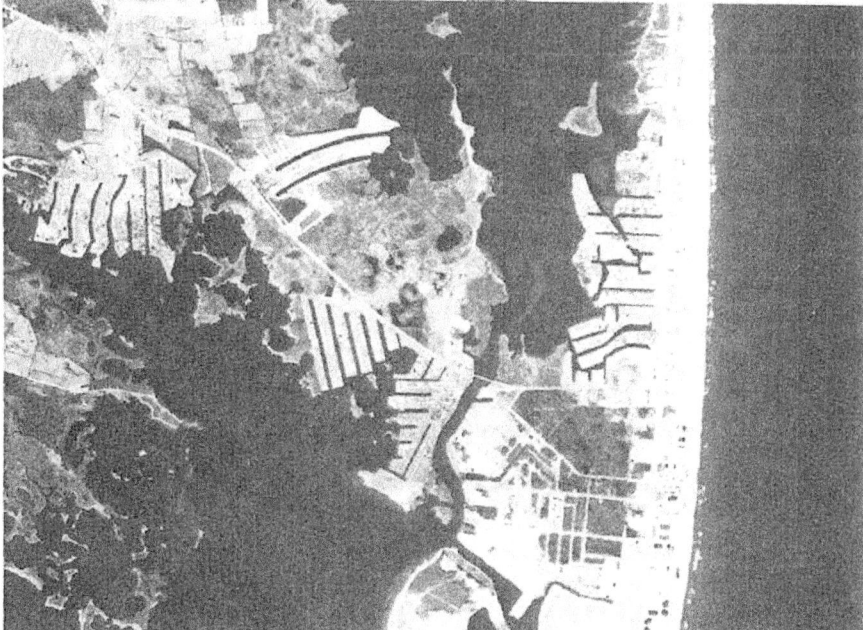

b

Human activities have had a greater impact on wetlands than natural events: (a) Fenwick Island—Bayville area of Delaware in 1954 and (b) same area in 1977. Note drastic decrease in coastal wetlands along bays by dredge and fill residential developments.

Current Status of Wetlands
DELAWARE

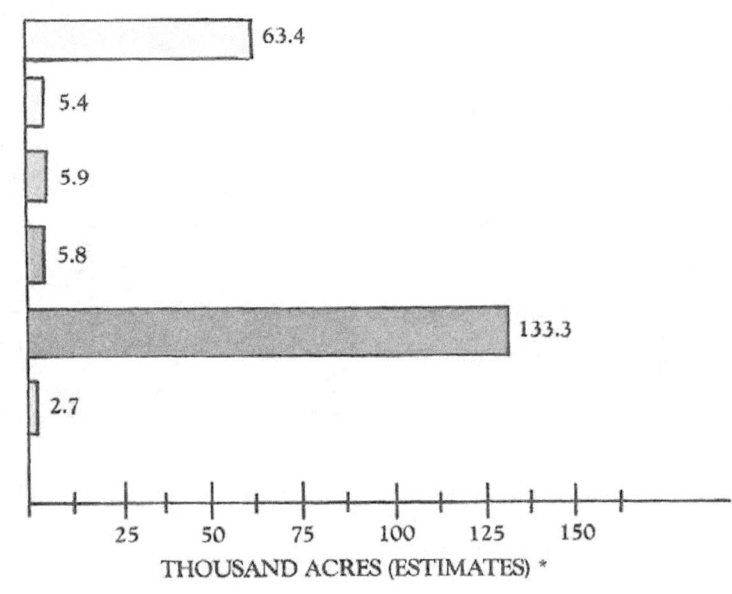

COASTAL MARSHES — 63.4

TIDAL FLATS/BEACHES — 5.4

INLAND EMERGENT WETLANDS — 5.9

INLAND SHRUB WETLANDS — 5.8

INLAND FORESTED WETLANDS — 133.3

FRESHWATER PONDS — 2.7

25 50 75 100 125 150

THOUSAND ACRES (ESTIMATES) *

*Actual wetland acreages are available in **Wetlands of Delaware**—a cooperative U.S. Fish and Wildlife Service and Delaware Department of Natural Resources and Environmental Control publication.

Roughly 216,000 acres of wetlands exist in Delaware. Coastal wetlands represent slightly less than one-third of the state's wetlands, while the majority are inland forested wetlands.

WETLAND DISTRIBUTION

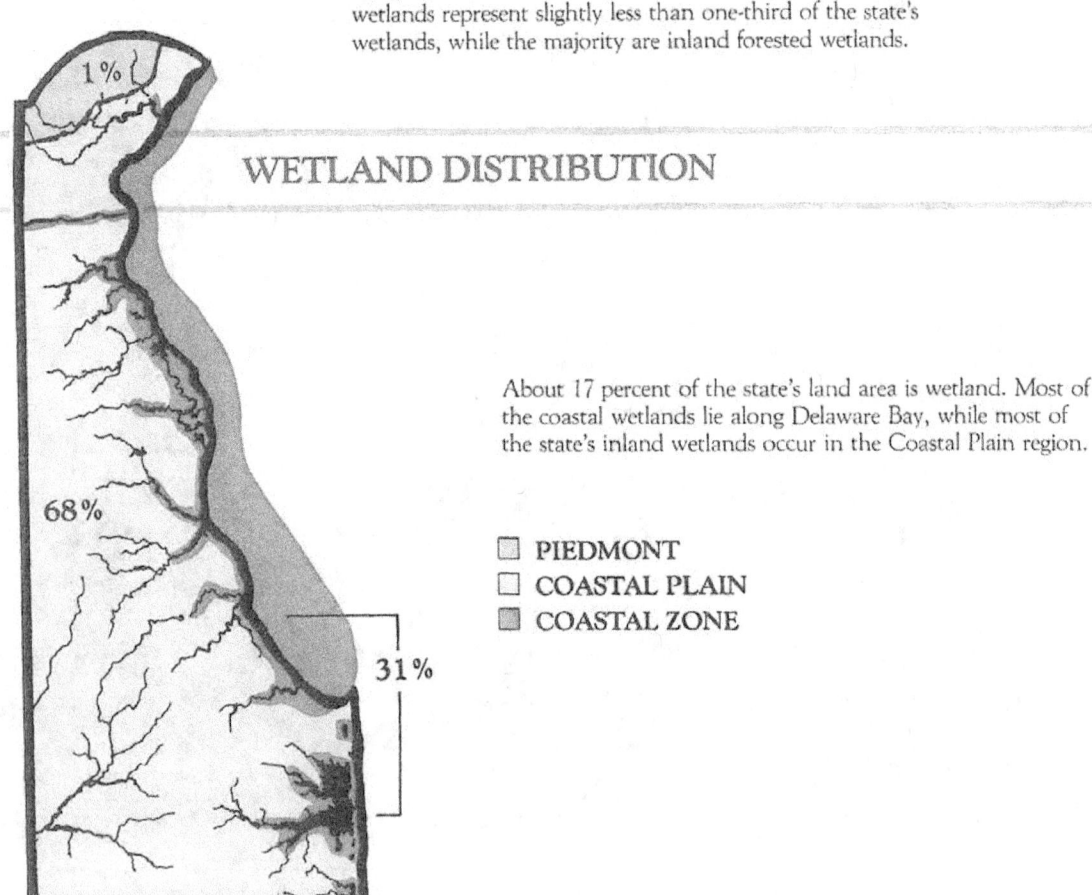

1 %

68%

31%

About 17 percent of the state's land area is wetland. Most of the coastal wetlands lie along Delaware Bay, while most of the state's inland wetlands occur in the Coastal Plain region.

☐ PIEDMONT
☐ COASTAL PLAIN
▨ COASTAL ZONE

Current Status of Wetlands
MARYLAND

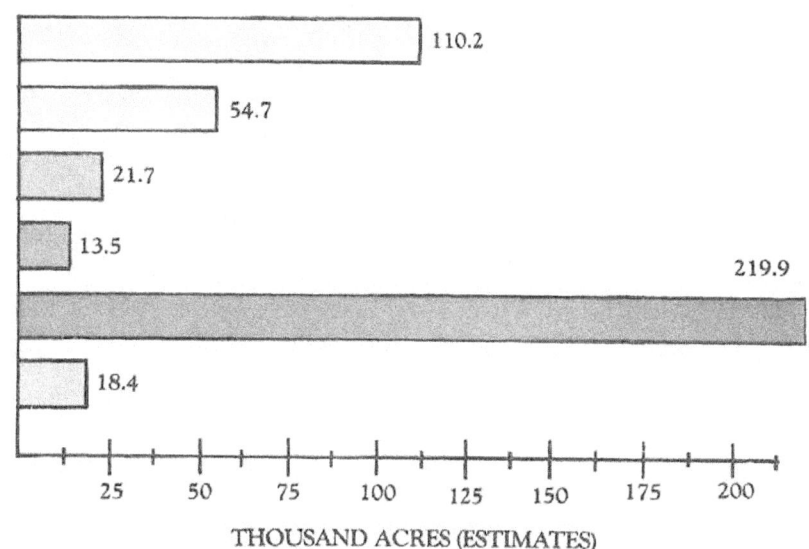

	THOUSAND ACRES (ESTIMATES)
COASTAL MARSHES	110.2
TIDAL FLATS/BEACHES	54.7
INLAND EMERGENT WETLANDS	21.7
INLAND SHRUB WETLANDS	13.5
INLAND FORESTED WETLANDS	219.9
FRESHWATER PONDS	18.4

Maryland possesses nearly 440,000 acres of wetlands. Inland wetlands represent nearly two-thirds of the state's wetlands, with coastal wetlands comprising the remainder.

WETLAND DISTRIBUTION

About six percent of the state's land area is represented by wetland. Forty-eight percent of the state's total wetlands and nearly 80 percent of its inland wetlands are associated with the Lower Coastal Plain area on the Eastern Shore. Coastal wetlands comprise about 38 percent of the state's wetlands and are mostly associated with Chesapeake Bay, with the rest found along the Atlantic Ocean behind Assateague Island.

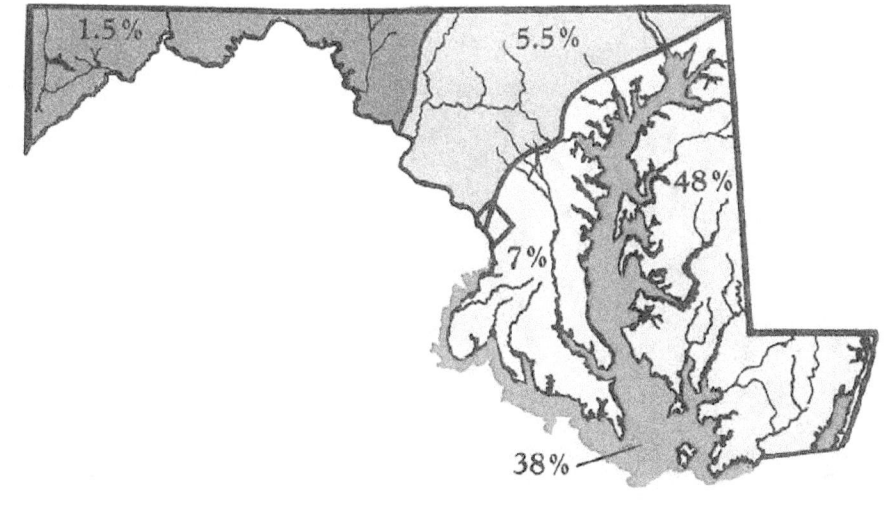

▨ APPALACHIAN HIGHLANDS
☐ PIEDMONT
☐ UPPER COASTAL PLAIN
☐ LOWER COASTAL PLAIN
▨ COASTAL ZONE

Current Status of Wetlands
PENNSYLVANIA

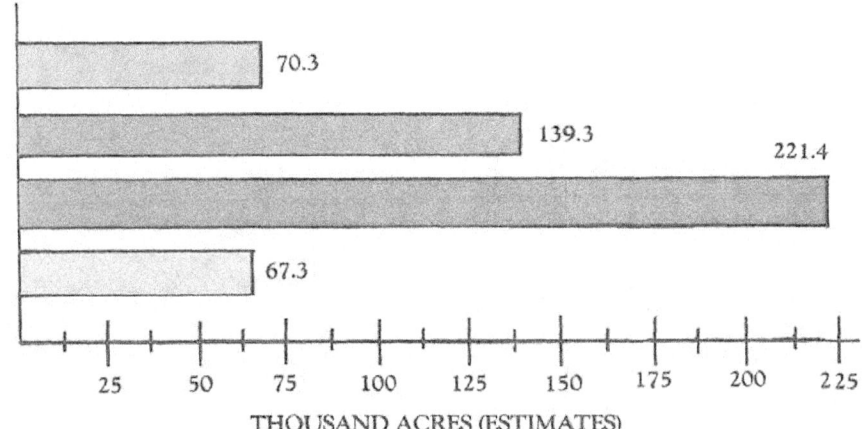

EMERGENT WETLANDS — 70.3

SHRUB WETLANDS — 139.3

FORESTED WETLANDS — 221.4

FRESHWATER PONDS — 67.3

THOUSAND ACRES (ESTIMATES)

Nearly one-half million acres of wetlands are present in Pennsylvania. Forested wetlands and shrub wetlands comprise slightly less than three-quarters of the state's wetlands.

WETLAND DISTRIBUTION

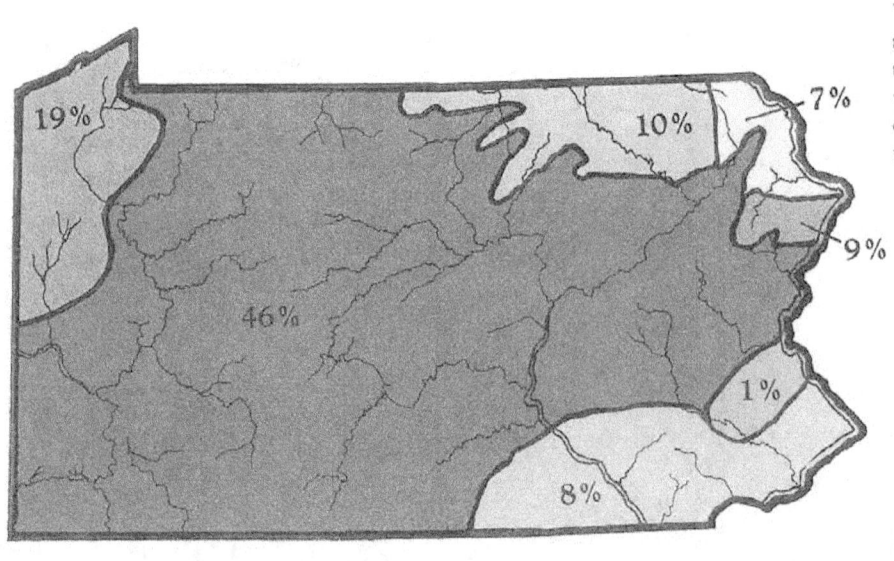

Wetlands represent about two percent of the state's land area. Nearly one-fifth of the state's wetlands are found in north-western Pennsylvania, while an almost equal amount is located in the Pocono region.

☐ MIDDLE WESTERN UPLAND PLAIN
■ APPALACHIAN HIGHLANDS
☐ OTHER GLACIATED NORTHEASTERN PENN *
☐ POCONOS #1 *
■ POCONOS #2 *
☐ PIEDMONT
☐ ADIRONDACK– NEW ENGLAND HIGHLANDS

*These areas are part of the Appalachian Highlands physiographic region.

Current Status of Wetlands
VIRGINIA

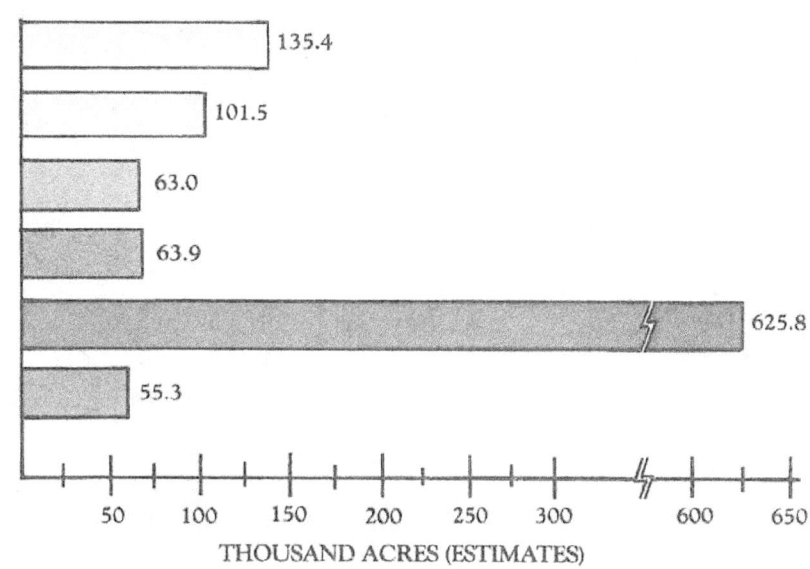

COASTAL MARSHES	135.4
TIDAL FLATS/BEACHES	101.5
INLAND EMERGENT WETLANDS	63.0
INLAND SHRUB WETLANDS	63.9
INLAND FORESTED WETLANDS	625.8
FRESHWATER PONDS	55.3

50   100   150   200   250   300   600   650

THOUSAND ACRES (ESTIMATES)

Virginia has slightly more than one million acres of wetlands.
Coastal wetlands represent slightly less than one-fourth of the
state's wetlands, while inland wetlands are most abundant.

WETLAND DISTRIBUTION

About four percent of the state's land area
is wetland. Most of Virginia's wetlands are
found in the Coastal Plain, where 64 percent of the state's freshwater wetlands are
located. The Piedmont has 22 percent of
the state's total wetlands which represents
28 percent of the state's freshwater
wetlands.

- ▨ APPALACHIAN HIGHLANDS
- ☐ PIEDMONT
- ☐ UPPER COASTAL PLAIN
- ☐ LOWER COASTAL PLAIN
- ▨ COASTAL ZONE

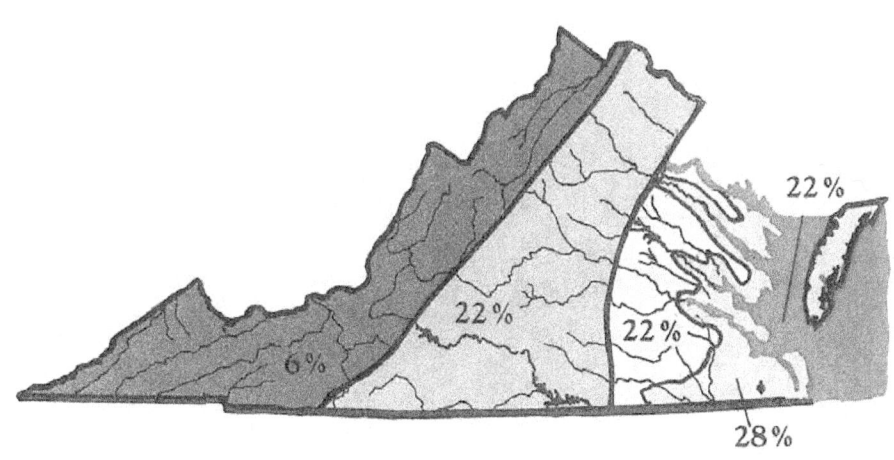

Current Status of Wetlands
WEST VIRGINIA

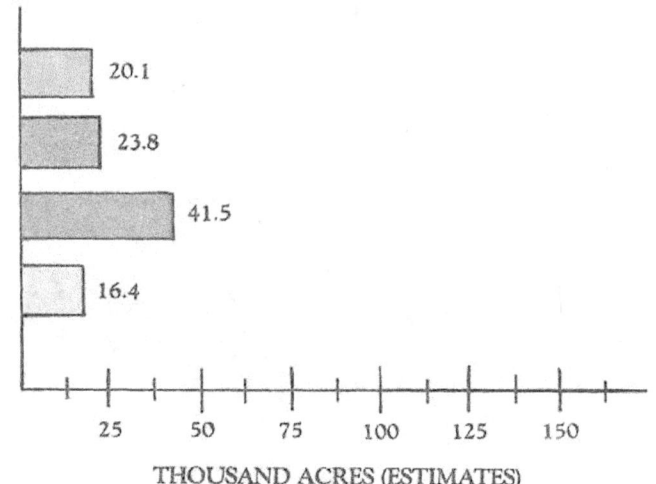

EMERGENT WETLANDS — 20.1

SHRUB WETLANDS — 23.8

FORESTED WETLANDS — 41.5

FRESHWATER PONDS — 16.4

THOUSAND ACRES (ESTIMATES)

Roughly 102,000 acres of wetlands are present in West Virginia. Forty-one percent of the state's wetlands are forested wetlands, with about equal amounts of emergent and shrub wetlands present.

WETLAND DISTRIBUTION

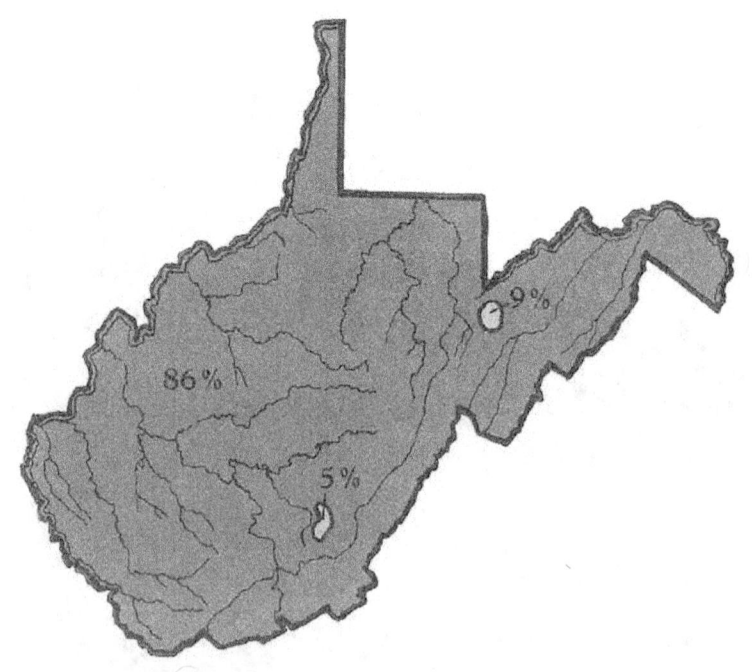

The Canaan Valley and the Meadow River area possess about 14 percent of the state's wetlands. Overall, less than one percent of West Virginia is wetland.

▨ APPALACHIAN HIGHLANDS
▢ CANAAN VALLEY *
▢ MEADOW RIVER AREA*

*These areas are part of the Appalachian Highlands physiographic region.

Current Status of Wetlands
CHESAPEAKE WATERSHED

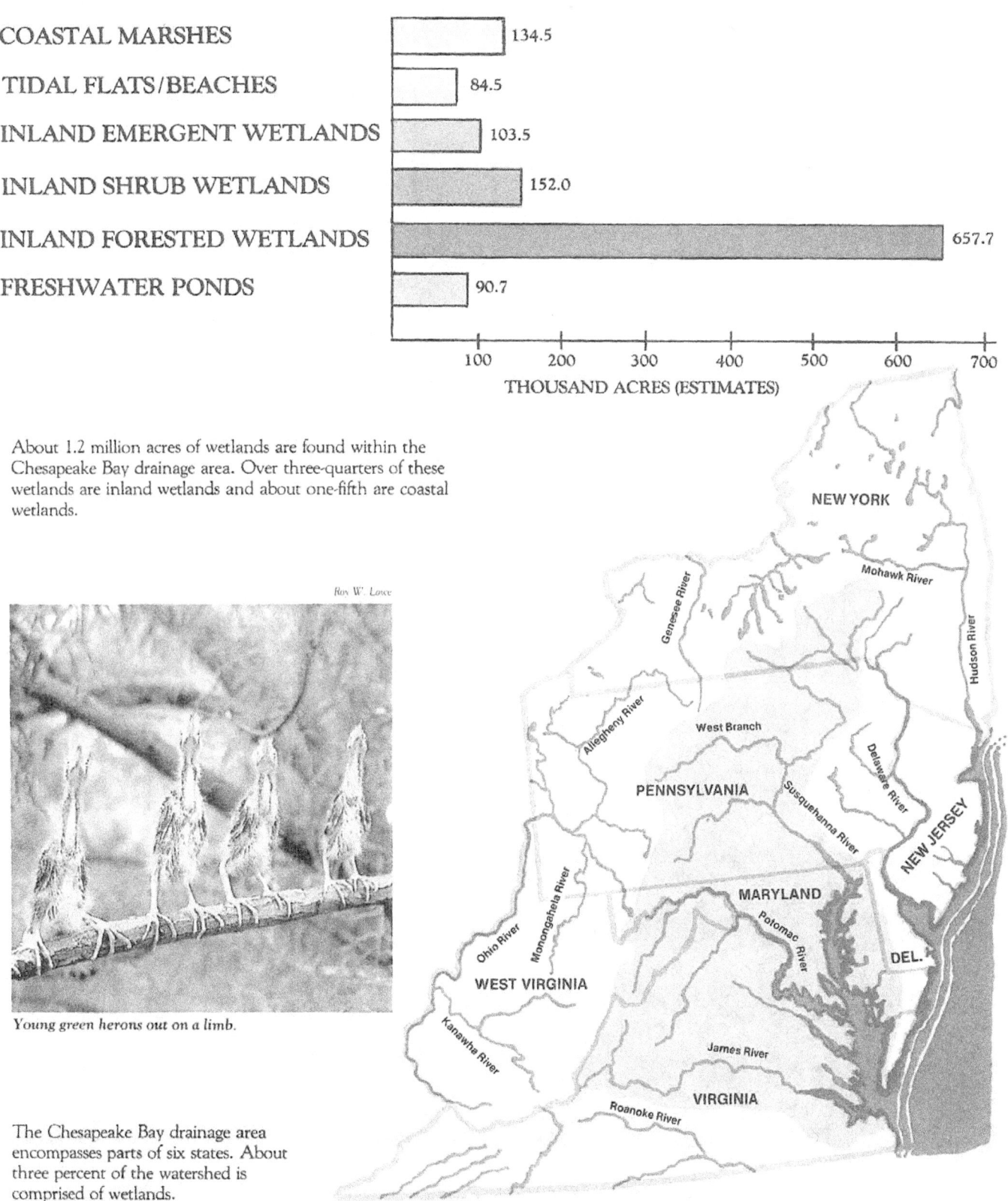

	Thousand Acres
COASTAL MARSHES	134.5
TIDAL FLATS/BEACHES	84.5
INLAND EMERGENT WETLANDS	103.5
INLAND SHRUB WETLANDS	152.0
INLAND FORESTED WETLANDS	657.7
FRESHWATER PONDS	90.7

THOUSAND ACRES (ESTIMATES)

About 1.2 million acres of wetlands are found within the Chesapeake Bay drainage area. Over three-quarters of these wetlands are inland wetlands and about one-fifth are coastal wetlands.

Roy W. Lowe

Young green herons out on a limb.

The Chesapeake Bay drainage area encompasses parts of six states. About three percent of the watershed is comprised of wetlands.

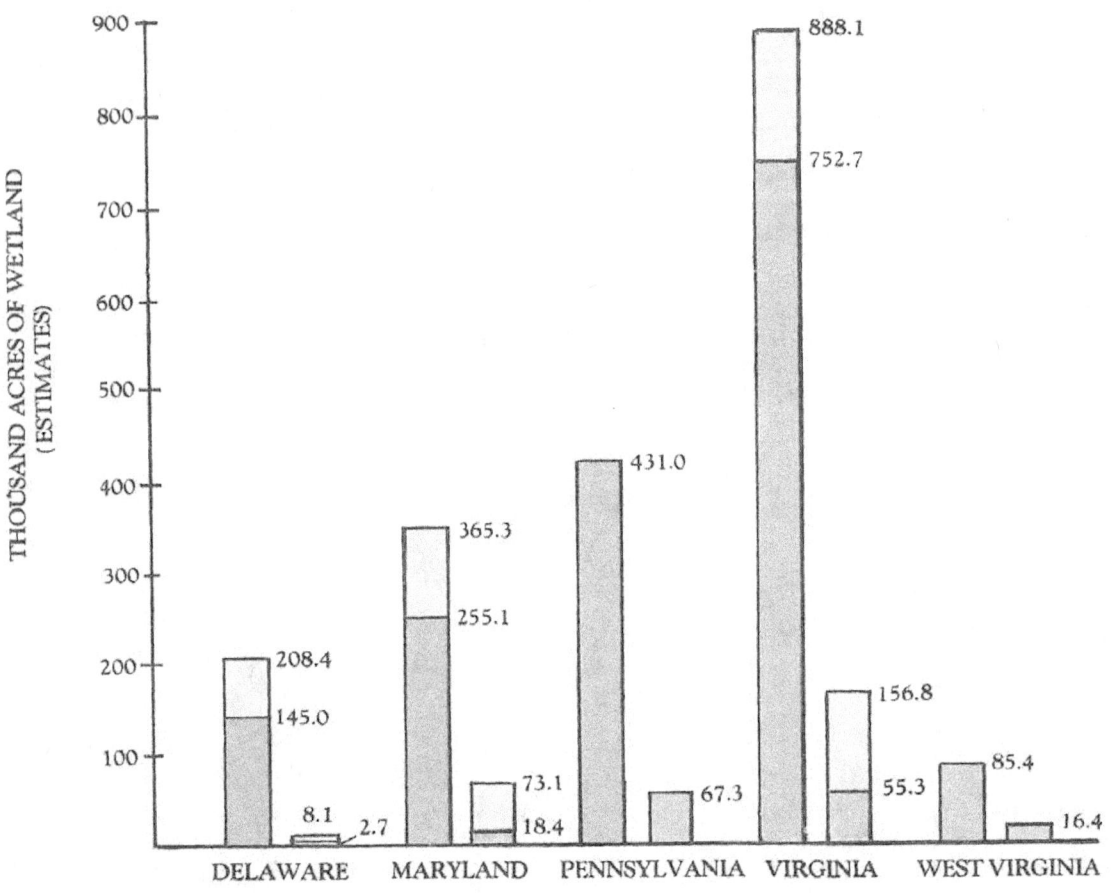

THOUSAND ACRES OF WETLAND (ESTIMATES)

DELAWARE — 208.4, 145.0, 8.1, 2.7

MARYLAND — 365.3, 255.1, 73.1, 18.4

PENNSYLVANIA — 431.0, 67.3

VIRGINIA — 888.1, 752.7, 156.8, 55.3

WEST VIRGINIA — 85.4, 55.3, 16.4

The five-state region has slightly more than two million acres of wetlands. This amounts to an area twice the size of Delaware or one-third of the size of Maryland. Virginia has the greatest wetland acreage among the five states, while mountainous West Virginia has the least.

☐ **INLAND VEGETATED WETLANDS**
☐ **COASTAL VEGETATED WETLANDS**
☐ **TIDAL FLATS/BEACHES***
☐ **FRESHWATER PONDS***

*Nonvegetated Wetlands

Seasonally flooded forested wetland.

Irregularly flooded coastal marsh.

Over half of the region's wetlands are located near the coast, where all of the coastal wetlands and about half of the inland wetlands are found. Virginia has almost half of the region's wetlands.

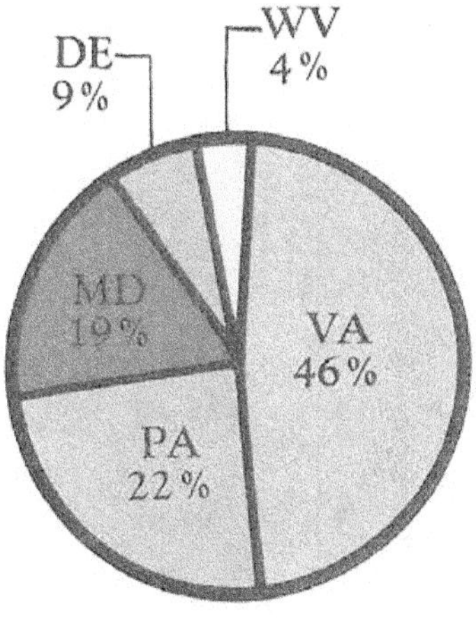

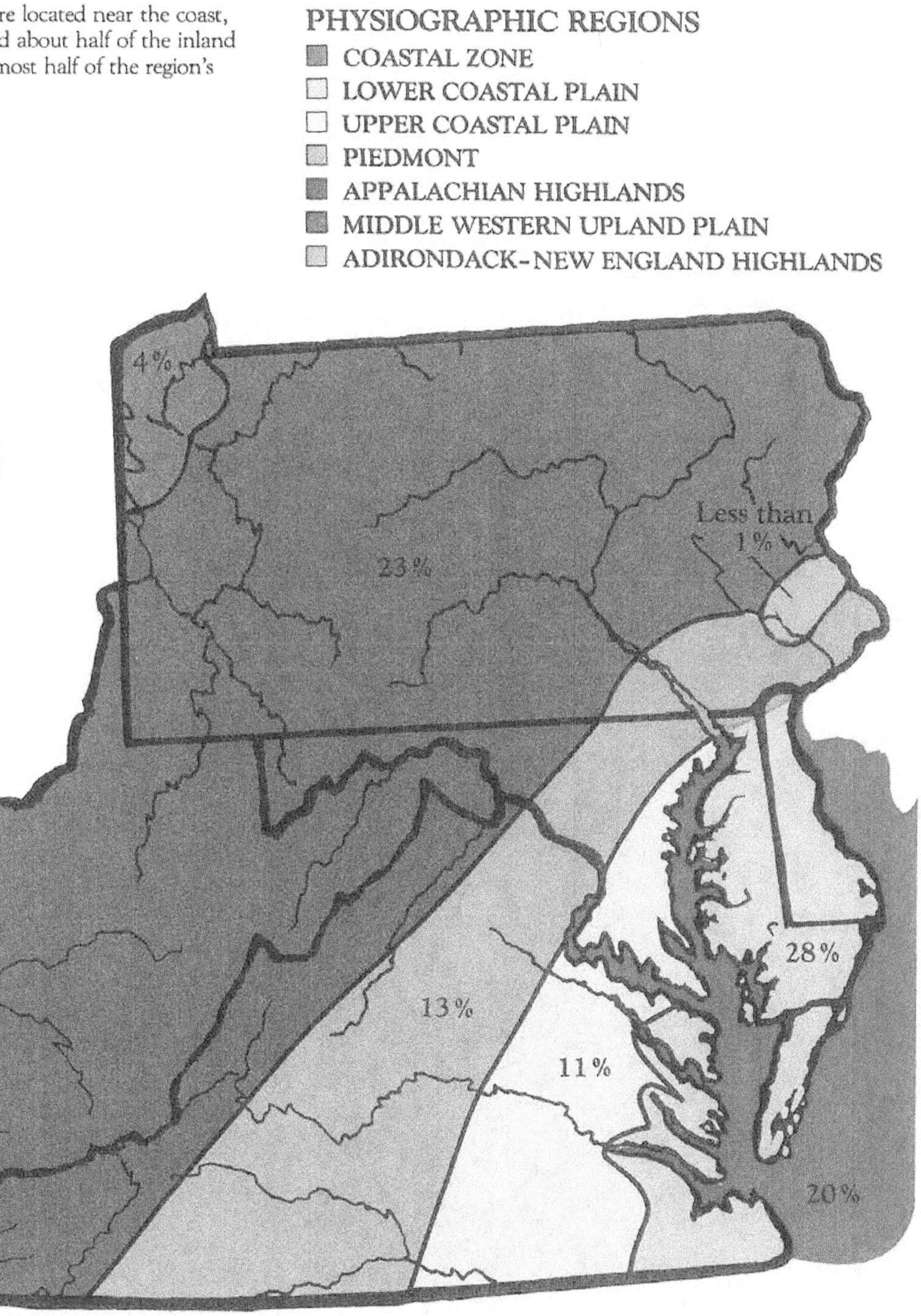

PHYSIOGRAPHIC REGIONS

- ▦ COASTAL ZONE
- ☐ LOWER COASTAL PLAIN
- ☐ UPPER COASTAL PLAIN
- ▨ PIEDMONT
- ▦ APPALACHIAN HIGHLANDS
- ▦ MIDDLE WESTERN UPLAND PLAIN
- ▨ ADIRONDACK–NEW ENGLAND HIGHLANDS

WV
4 %

DE
9 %

MD
19 %

VA
46 %

PA
22 %

**Wetland Distribution
By State**

4 %

23 %

Less than
1 %

28 %

13 %

11 %

20 %

Wetland Distribution By Physiographic Region

15

RECENT WETLAND TRENDS

Wetlands are changing natural environments subjected to both human-induced and natural forces. These forces result in wetland gains and losses and affect the quality of the remaining wetlands. Major causes of wetland change are outlined below:

Human-induced Actions

1. Agriculture—draining and clearing wetlands for crop production.
2. Pond and lake construction—impounding or excavating and flooding wetlands for water supply, flood protection, recreation, and other purposes.
3. Urban development—filling wetlands for houses, industrial facilities, ports, commercial buildings, highways, waste disposal, airports, and other purposes.
4. Other development—mainly dredging or channelizing (excavating) wetlands for navigation and flood protection which often facilitates timber harvest or wetland conversion to farmland and urbanland; silviculture; peat, coal, sand and gravel mining and oil and gas extraction to lesser extents; and altering natural drainage patterns.
5. Coastal impoundment construction—diking and flooding coastal wetlands to create brackish water impoundments for waterfowl use or other purposes.
6. Pollution—degrading the quality of wetlands by direct or indirect discharge of various materials including pesticides, herbicides, other chemicals, sediment, domestic sewage, and agricultural wastes.

Natural Forces

1. Subsidence of coastal areas related to rising sea level.
2. Natural succession from one wetland type to another.
3. Erosion and accretion.

Rick Newton

A serious threat to wetlands is excavation and filling operations.

Ralph Tiner

Urban development of wetlands destroys natural values.

Bill Zinni

Ditching wetlands alters natural drainage patterns and may significantly change wetland functions.

USFWS

Channelization projects often accelerate conversion of wetlands to farmlands.

4. Animal actions—e.g., beaver impoundments and muskrat and goose "eat-outs."
5. Droughts.
6. Hurricanes and other major storms.

Human actions are particularly significant in determining the fate of wetlands. Unfortunately, many human activities are destructive to wetlands, either converting them to agricultural or other lands or degrading their quality by pollution. A few actions do, however, create wetlands. Construction of farm ponds in upland areas may increase wetland acreage. Restoration of previously drained wetlands can also be beneficial. Wetland protection efforts serve to help maintain and enhance our wetland resources, despite mounting pressures to convert them to other uses.

The best available estimates for recent wetland changes in the five states and the Chesapeake Bay watershed are illustrated on the following pages.

Ralph Tiner a

Kelly Drake

Wetlands are still being used by some people to dispose of waste products.

Some wetlands are particularly vulnerable to agricultural conversion during dry periods. Wet meadow of soft rush before (a) and after plowing (b). b

Wetland Trends
DELAWARE

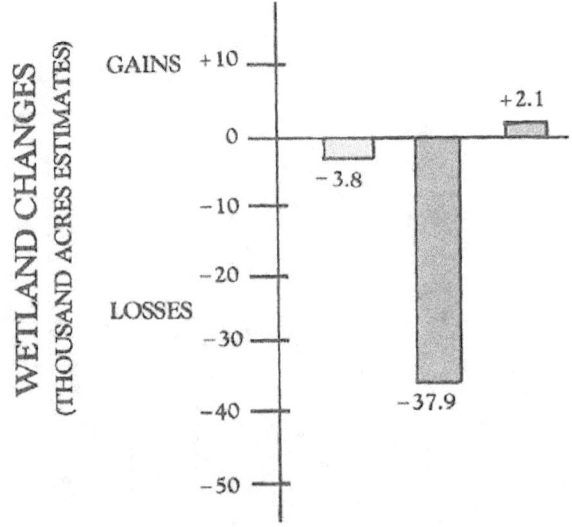

WETLAND CHANGES
(THOUSAND ACRES ESTIMATES)

GAINS +10

0

-3.8

-10

-20

LOSSES

-30

-37.9

-40

-50

+2.1

☐ COASTAL WETLANDS
☐ INLAND VEGETATED WETLANDS
☐ FRESHWATER PONDS

Between 1955 and 1981, Delaware lost about 42,000 acres of coastal wetlands and inland vegetated wetlands, for an average annual loss of 1,600 acres. During this time, pond acreage increased by 2,000 acres for a 400 percent gain. The vast majority of the wetland losses involved inland wetlands, particularly forested wetlands which decreased by about 17 percent. Statewide, 21 percent of Delaware's inland vegetated wetlands and six percent of its coastal wetlands recently disappeared.

CAUSES OF INLAND VEGETATED WETLAND LOSSES

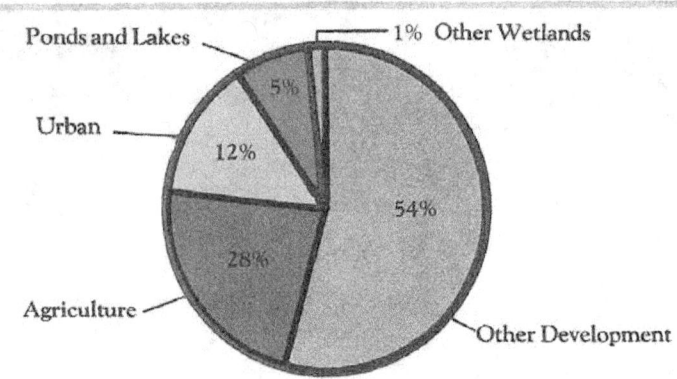

Ponds and Lakes
1% Other Wetlands
5%
Urban
12%
54%
28%
Agriculture
Other Development

Other development, mainly channelization and ditching projects related to agriculture, were responsible for over 50 percent of the recent losses of inland marshes and swamps. Direct conversion of wetland to farmland caused 28 percent of the losses.

CAUSES OF COASTAL WETLAND LOSSES

Urban development of coastal wetlands caused almost two-thirds of the state's losses of these wetlands. Many coastal wetlands were also converted to coastal waters by coastal impoundments, dredging projects, and rising sea level.

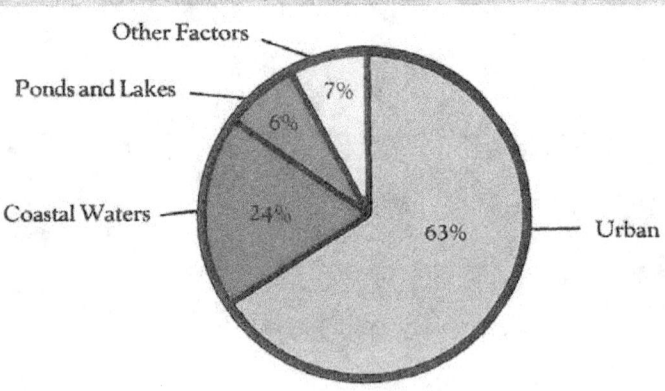

Other Factors
Ponds and Lakes
7%
6%
Coastal Waters
24%
63%
Urban

Wetland Trends
MARYLAND

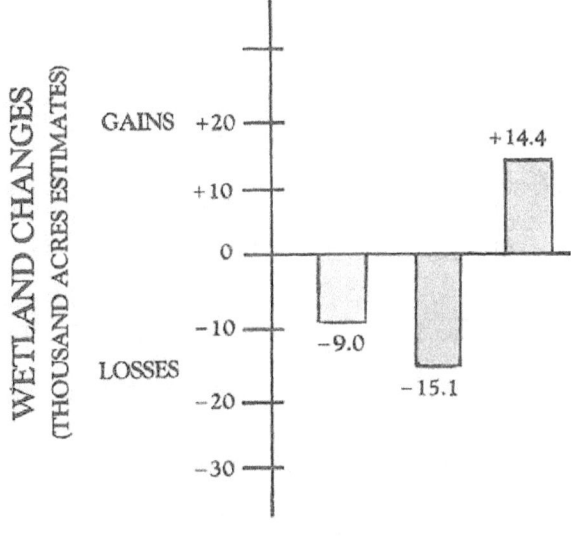

WETLAND CHANGES (THOUSAND ACRES ESTIMATES)

GAINS +20

+10

0

−10

LOSSES

−20

−30

−9.0

−15.1

+14.4

☐ COASTAL WETLANDS
▨ INLAND VEGETATED WETLANDS
▤ FRESHWATER PONDS

Between 1955 and 1978, about 24,000 acres of Maryland's coastal wetlands and inland vegetated wetlands disappeared, representing a five percent loss. Annual losses of these wetlands averaged about 1,000 acres. Inland vegetated wetlands decreased by six percent, while coastal vegetated wetlands fell by slightly more than eight percent. Roughly 91 percent of the inland vegetated wetland losses occurred in the Lower Coastal Plain region. Coastal and inland emergent wetlands were the most threatened types. In contrast to these losses, pond acreage increased by about 365 percent.

CAUSES OF INLAND VEGETATED WETLAND LOSSES

Other development (mostly channelization and ditching projects related to farmland) and agriculture caused nearly two-thirds of Maryland's recent loss of inland vegetated wetlands. Pond and lake construction was responsible for slightly more than one-quarter of the losses, while urban development caused eight percent of the losses.

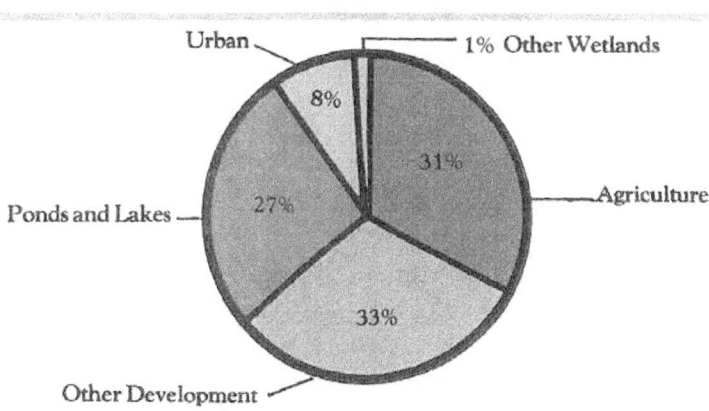

Urban — 8%
1% Other Wetlands
31% — Agriculture
Ponds and Lakes — 27%
33%
Other Development

CAUSES OF COASTAL WETLAND LOSSES

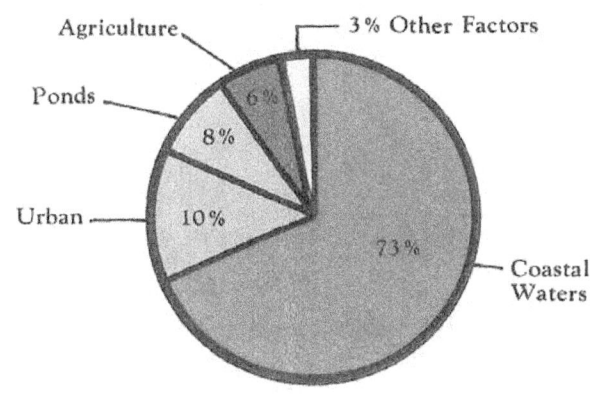

Agriculture — 6%
3% Other Factors
Ponds — 8%
Urban — 10%
73% — Coastal Waters

Almost three-quarters of the loss of Maryland's coastal wetlands was the result of coastal impoundments, dredging projects, and rising sea level. Filling for urban development caused ten percent of the losses.

19

Wetland Trends
PENNSYLVANIA

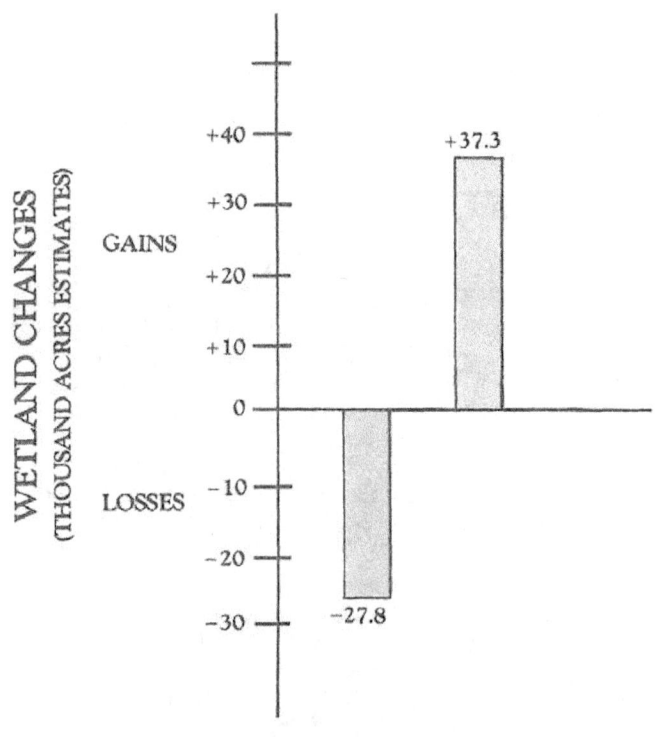

WETLAND CHANGES
(THOUSAND ACRES ESTIMATES)

GAINS

LOSSES

+37.3

−27.8

☐ INLAND VEGETATED WETLANDS
☐ FRESHWATER PONDS

Between 1956 and 1979, Pennsylvania experienced a net loss of nearly 28,000 acres of inland vegetated wetlands, for a six percent loss. Over 1,200 acres were lost annually, on average. Emergent wetlands were hardest hit with a 38 percent loss. Vegetated wetland losses were greatest in the northern section of the Pocono region which lost 15 percent of its wetlands. Pond acreage recently increased by about 130 percent.

CAUSES OF INLAND VEGETATED WETLAND LOSSES

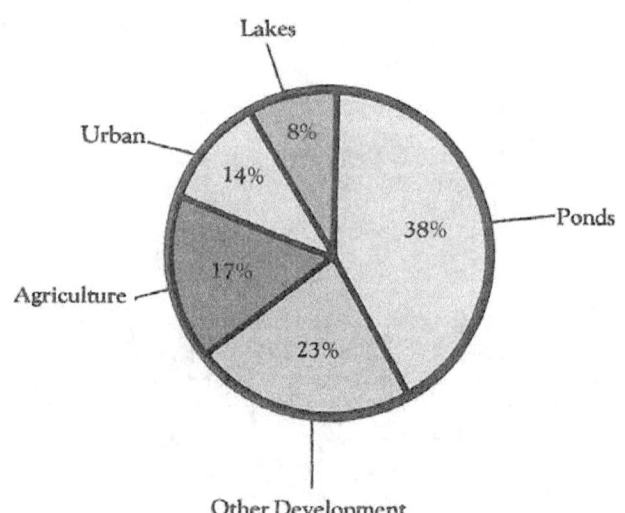

Lakes

Urban

Agriculture

Ponds

Other Development

8%

14%

17%

23%

38%

Pond construction was the greatest cause of vegetated wetland loss in Pennsylvania. Other development (including channelization and peat mining) was responsible for nearly a quarter of the recent losses. Peat mining in the Pocono region may also be responsible for a considerable amount of the losses due to pond and lake construction.

Randy Pomponio

Peat mining in the Poconos.

Wetland Trends
VIRGINIA

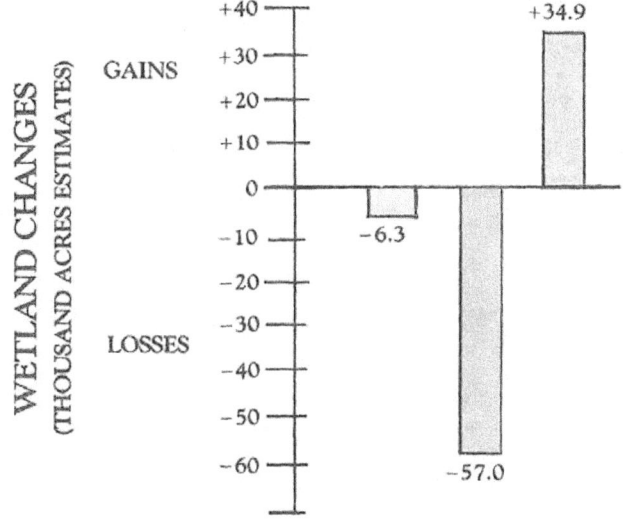

WETLAND CHANGES (THOUSAND ACRES ESTIMATES)

GAINS

LOSSES

+34.9

-6.3

-57.0

☐ COASTAL WETLANDS
☐ INLAND VEGETATED WETLANDS
☐ FRESHWATER PONDS

Between 1956 and 1977, over 63,000 acres of Virginia's coastal wetlands and inland vegetated wetlands were lost, for a six percent loss. Annual losses of these wetlands averaged about 3,000 acres. Inland forested wetlands were most threatened, experiencing a nine percent loss in 21 years. Inland vegetated wetland loss was greatest in the Lower Coastal Plain region where about 14 percent of these wetlands were destroyed. Losses in this region accounted for 80 percent of the state's inland vegetated wetland losses. In stark contrast to other wetland losses, pond acreage increased by about 170 percent.

CAUSES OF INLAND VEGETATED WETLAND LOSSES

Direct conversion of wetlands to cropland was the major cause of inland wetland loss, while other development (mainly channelization projects) and lake and pond construction were also major loss factors.

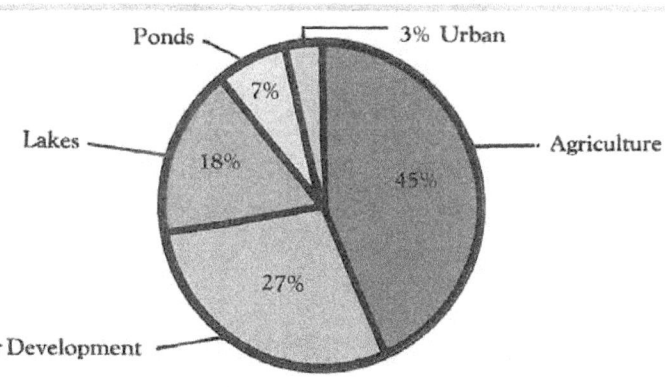

Ponds
7%

3% Urban

Lakes
18%

Agriculture
45%

Other Development
27%

CAUSES OF COASTAL WETLAND LOSSES

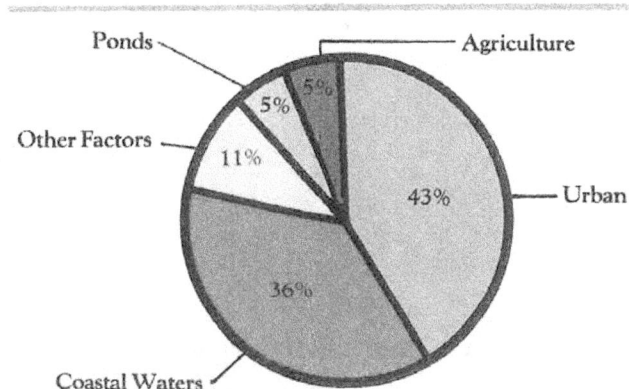

Ponds
5%

Agriculture
5%

Other Factors
11%

Urban
43%

Coastal Waters
36%

Urban development had the biggest impact on coastal wetlands. Loss of coastal wetland to estuarine waters through impoundments, dredging projects, and sea level rise was also significant.

Wetland Trends
WEST VIRGINIA

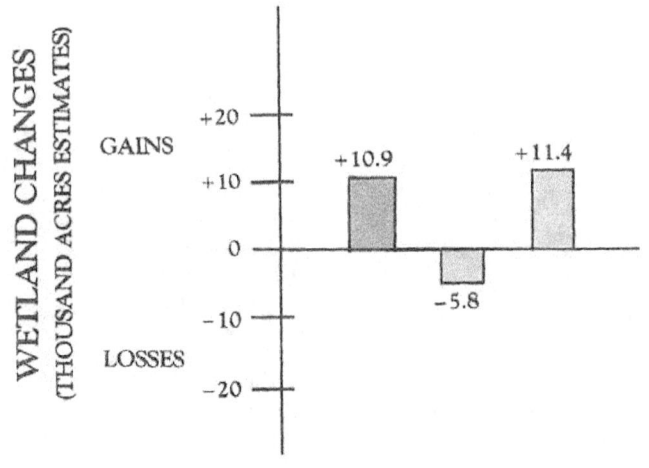

WETLAND CHANGES (THOUSAND ACRES ESTIMATES)

GAINS

LOSSES

+20

+10

0

−10

−20

+10.9

−5.8

+11.4

▨ FORESTED AND SHRUB WETLANDS
▧ EMERGENT WETLANDS
▫ FRESHWATER PONDS

Best available estimates of West Virginia wetland trends for 1957 to 1980 suggest: (1) nearly a 6,000 acre loss of emergent wetlands which amounts to a 22 percent loss and (2) an increase in forested and shrub wetlands and freshwater ponds. Most of the emergent wetland loss was to shrub wetlands, accounting for much of the gain in this type, while forested wetlands increased largely at the expense of shrub wetlands. Pond acreage increased by about 225 percent.

CAUSES OF INLAND VEGETATED WETLAND LOSSES

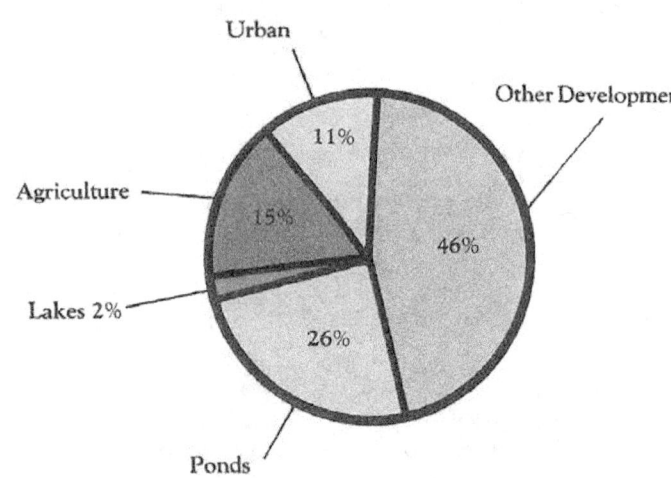

Urban

Other Development

Agriculture

Lakes 2%

Ponds

11%

15%

46%

26%

Other development (including channelization projects) was largely responsible for recent losses of West Virginia's wetlands. Pond construction in wetlands was also significant.

Wetland Trends
CHESAPEAKE WATERSHED

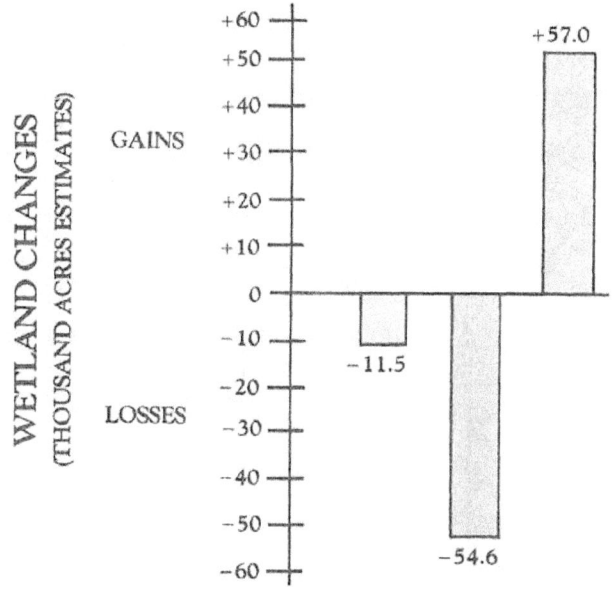

GAINS

LOSSES

+60
+50
+40
+30
+20
+10
0
-10
-20
-30
-40
-50
-60

+57.0

-11.5

-54.6

☐ COASTAL WETLANDS
☐ INLAND VEGETATED WETLANDS
☐ FRESHWATER PONDS

The Chesapeake Bay watershed experienced substantial losses of coastal wetlands and inland vegetated wetlands between the mid-1950's and late 1970's. Annual losses of these types averaged over 2,800 acres. Coastal marshes declined by about nine percent, while inland vegetated wetlands fell by six percent. Coastal and inland emergent wetlands were the most threatened types in the basin. Recently, pond acreage increased by nearly 170 percent.

CAUSES OF INLAND VEGETATED WETLAND LOSSES

Agriculture and other development (mainly channelization related to farming) were equally responsible for nearly 60 percent of the inland vegetated wetland losses. Pond and lake construction was also significant, whereas urban development had less impact.

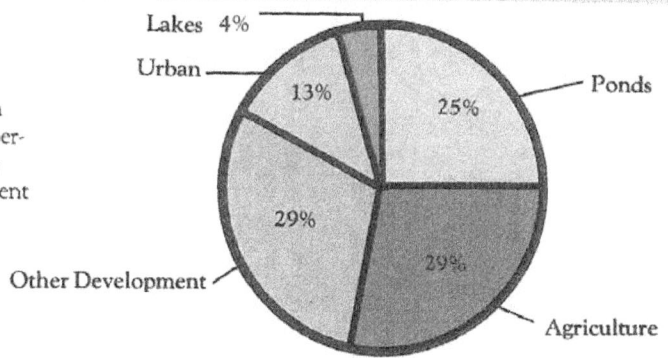

Lakes 4%
Urban
13%
Ponds
25%
Other Development
29%
29%
Agriculture

CAUSES OF COASTAL WETLAND LOSSES

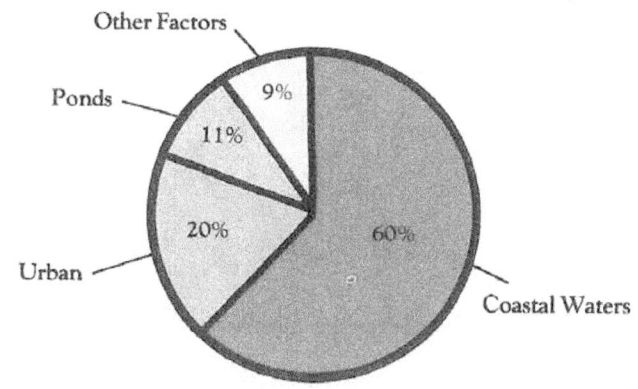

Other Factors
9%
Ponds
11%
Urban
20%
60%
Coastal Waters

Loss of coastal wetlands to estuarine waters was the most significant factor. This resulted from a combination of human and natural actions, including coastal impoundments, dredging projects, and the natural rise of sea level. Urban development was responsible for about one-fifth of the coastal wetland losses. Coastal wetlands experienced heavy losses prior to the early 1970's, before federal and state laws were enacted to control development of these wetlands.

WETLAND CHANGES (THOUSAND ACRES ESTIMATES)

GAINS

LOSSES

DE −3.8	VA −6.3	MD −9.0	WV +5.1	MD −15.1	PA −27.8	DE −37.9	VA −57.0	DE +2.1	WV +11.4	MD +14.4	VA +34.9	PA +37.3

- ■ COASTAL WETLAND LOSS
- □ INLAND VEGETATED WETLAND GAIN
- □ INLAND VEGETATED WETLAND LOSS
- □ FRESHWATER POND GAIN

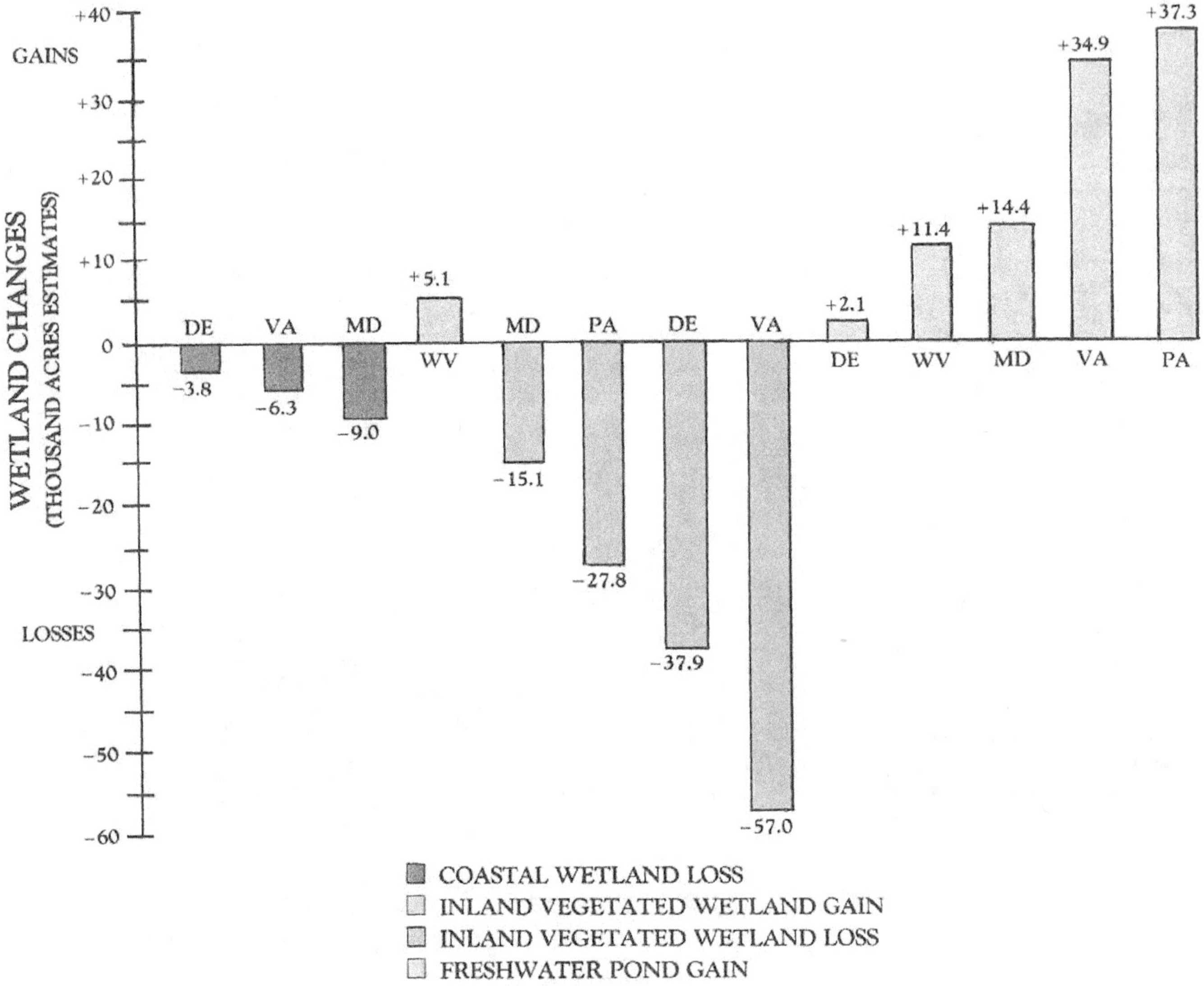

Between the mid-1950's and the late 1970's, the five-state region lost seven percent of its inland vegetated wetlands and six percent of its coastal marshes. The loss of about 133,000 acres of inland vegetated wetlands amounts to an area one-tenth of the size of Delaware or three times the size of Washington, D.C. Virginia experienced the greatest recent losses of inland vegetated wetlands, while coastal wetlands were most threatened in Maryland. Delaware lost the highest percentage (21 percent) of inland vegetated wetlands. West Virginia was the only state with an estimated increased in vegetated wetlands. Pennsylvania had the biggest gain in freshwater ponds.

15% Loss of Vegetated Wetlands in this area, accounting for 19% of Pennsylvania's Losses.

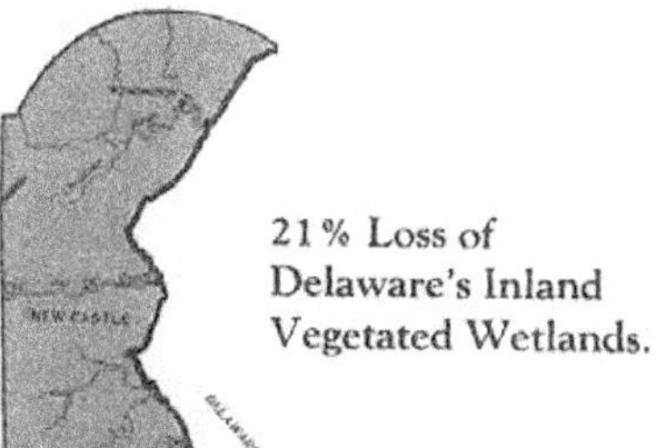

21% Loss of Delaware's Inland Vegetated Wetlands.

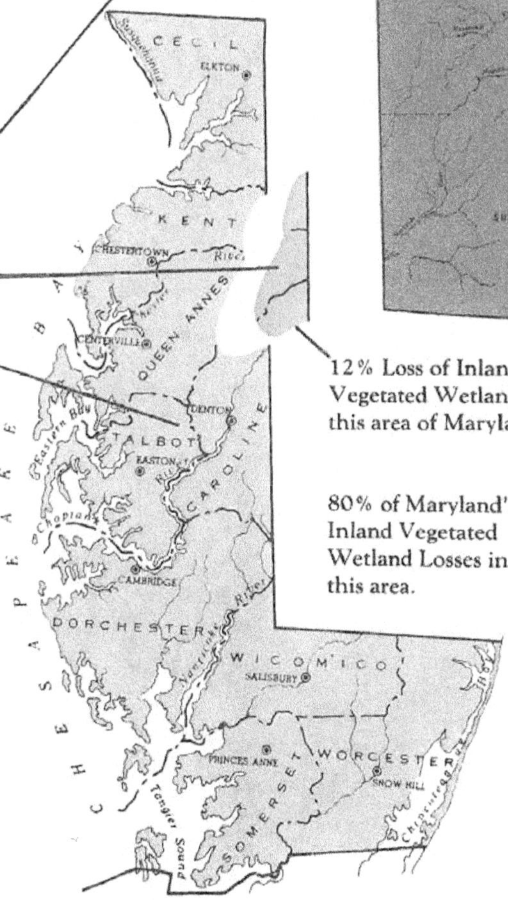

12% Loss of Inland Vegetated Wetlands in this area of Maryland.

80% of Maryland's Inland Vegetated Wetland Losses in this area.

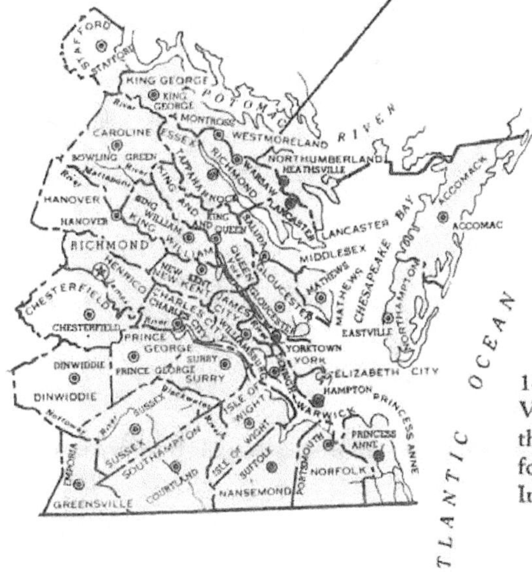

14% Loss of Inland Vegetated Wetlands in this area, accounting for 80% of Virginia's Inland Wetland Losses

Inland vegetated wetland losses were heaviest in the Lower Coastal Plain area where nearly three-quarters of the five-state region's losses took place. Agricultural conversion of these wetlands and associated channelization projects were the major reasons for these changes.

THE FUTURE OF MID-ATLANTIC WETLANDS

We have seen that significant wetland losses have recently taken place in the Mid-Atlantic region. We know that they represent losses of valuable natural resources and not simply losses of wastelands as once believed. So, what is being done to protect our remaining wetlands? In general, there are two widely used approaches to wetland protection: (1) acquisition of wetlands and (2) regulation of wetland uses. Acquisition involves purchasing wetlands or easements on wetlands and establishing wildlife refuges, sanctuaries, or conservation areas. This approach is used by government agencies and private conservation organizations. Funding for these efforts, however, is limited and we cannot expect that all of the remaining wetlands can be protected by acquisition. Regulations that control various uses of wetlands are, therefore, vital to protecting wetlands and saving the values they provide. Federal, state, and local governments may, through existing laws or ordinances, require that anyone planning construction or other development activities in wetlands obtain a permit or other approvals prior to initiating work. In the 1970's, several Mid-Atlantic states and the federal government enacted laws to regulate wetland uses. For the most part, however, these laws are not comprehensive in scope, since they may regulate only a specified number of activities adversely impacting wetlands and/or apply to only certain wetland types. For example, normal agricultural activities are exempt from most regulatory requirements. At the federal level, the U.S. Army Corps of Engineers regulates wetland uses to varying degrees. For inland wetlands, the deposition of fill material often requires a federal permit, while excavation of wetlands is generally exempted from permit requirements. Filling of coastal wetlands is also regulated and excavation in these wetlands may require a permit under certain circumstances. At the state level, Pennsylvania is the only Mid-Atlantic state to have statewide wetland regulations. Delaware, Maryland, and Virginia have laws to protect coastal wetlands which have significantly reduced losses of these wetlands, but they have no similar protection for inland wetlands. Despite the best efforts of the existing regulations, wetland losses, especially of inland wetlands, will continue as our population increases and demand for food, timber, and real estate rises. Even if losses were controlled, the problem of degrading the quality of wetlands through pollution, urban encroachment, partial drainage and other actions still needs to be addressed.

What can be done to slow the rate of wetland loss and to improve the quality of our remaining wetlands? Many opportunities exist for private citizens, corporations, government agencies, and others to help accomplish these objectives. Cooperation between public agencies and private citizens and the private sector is essential to securing a promising future for our wetlands. Individual landowners and corporations are in a key position to determine the fate of wetlands on their properties. Every citizen, landowner or not, can help wetlands by supporting any number of wetland conservation initiatives. Major public and private options for improving the status of wetlands are listed below:

PUBLIC OPTIONS:

1. Develop a consistent public policy to protect wetlands of national, state, and local significance.
2. Strengthen federal, state and local wetland protection.
3. Ensure proper implementation of existing laws and policies through adequate staffing, surveillance, enforcement, and training.
4. Increase wetland acquisition in selected areas for preservation purposes.
5. Remove government subsidies that encourage wetland drainage and destruction.

Ralph Tiner

Wetlands are valuable resources—natural treasures.

6. Provide tax and other incentives to private landowners and industry to promote wetland preservation and remove existing tax benefits that encourage wetland destruction.

7. Scrutinize cost-benefit analyses and justifications for flood control projects that involve channelization of wetlands and watercourses.

8. Improve wetland management on publicly-owned lands.

9. Increase the number of marsh creation and restoration projects (including enhancement of existing wetlands by improving local water quality and establishing buffer zones), especially related to mitigation for unavoidable wetland losses by government-sponsored water resource projects.

10. Monitor wetland changes especially with reference to the effectiveness of state and federal wetland protection efforts and periodically update the National Wetlands Inventory mapping in problem areas.

11. Increase public awareness of wetland values and the status of wetlands through various media.

12. Conduct research to increase our knowledge of wetland values and to identify ways of using wetlands that are least disruptive to their ecology and public values.

PRIVATE OPTIONS:

1. Rather than drain or fill wetlands, seek compatible uses involving minimal wetland alteration, such as selective timber harvest, waterfowl production, fur harvest, hay and forage, wild rice production, and hunting and trapping leases.

2. Seek non-wetland sites for development projects and avoid wetland alteration or degradation during project construction.

3. Donate wetlands or funds for purchasing wetlands to private or public conservation agencies.

4. Maintain wetlands as open space.

5. Work in concert with government agencies to inform the public about wetland values.

6. Construct ponds in uplands and manage for wetland and aquatic species.

7. Purchase federal and state duck stamps to support wetland acquisition.

8. Support various wetland conservation initiatives by public agencies and private organizations.

Wetlands are an important part of our national heritage. In many ways, they are diamonds-in-the-rough. Our quality of life is largely dependent on our nation's wealth of natural resources and wetlands are the vital link between our land and water resources. Serious attention must be given to minimizing adverse wetland impacts in our efforts to improve our economic and personal well-being. As wetlands are lost, the remaining wetlands become even more valuable. We have already lost over half of our nation's wetlands since America was first settled. We must now take positive steps to protect wetlands to ensure that the values they now provide will be preserved for future generations.

Ralph Tiner

Kelly Drake

Options for the future—the choice is ours.

ACKNOWLEDGEMENTS

Many people have contributed to the publication of this document. Jim Butch (EPA-Region III) served as project officer and provided comments on the draft manuscript. Other reviewers included Dr. Jack Finn (University of Massachusetts), Dr. Gregor Auble, Inez Connor, Charles Kulp, Dr. Bill Wilen, Dr. Donald Woodard, and Bill Zinni (FWS), Bill Hoffman, Nels Barrett, Patty Weber, and Randy Pomponio (EPA), David Hardin (formerly Delaware Dept. of Natural Resources and Environmental Control), Khervin Smith and Shamus Malone (Pennsylvania Dept. of Environmental Resources), Harold Cassell (Maryland Water Resources Administration), Norman Larsen (Virginia Marine Resources Commission), and Dr. Gene Silberhorn (Virginia Institute of Marine Science).

Information on wetland status and trends for this region was largely the result of the diligent efforts of photo interpreters and cartographers at the Department of Forestry and Wildlife Management, University of Massachusetts, Amherst, especially: John LeBlanc, Gail Shaughnessy, Edwin Howes, Maria Mpelkes, Michael Broschart, Lawrence Oliver, David Wilkie, Dennis Swartwout, and Amy Hogeland. Lynn Hayes and Joanne Kalin (FWS) assisted by typing final and draft manuscripts, respectively. Mary O'Connor and Libby Hopkins helped with graphics support. This booklet was designed and illustrated by Wayne Geehan. The efforts of these people and others are greatly appreciated.

FOR INFORMATION ON FEDERAL AND STATE WETLAND REGULATIONS CONTACT THE FOLLOWING AGENCIES:

FEDERAL

U.S. Environmental Protection Agency
Wetlands and Marine Policy Section
841 Chestnut Building
Philadelphia, PA 19107
(215) 597-1182

U.S. Army Corps of Engineers

District Engineer
Baltimore District,
Corps of Engineers
P.O. Box 1715
Baltimore, MD 21203
(301) 962-3670

District Engineer
Philadelphia District,
Corps of Engineers
Custom House,
2nd & Chestnut Streets
Philadelphia, PA 19106
(215) 597-2812

District Engineer
Pittsburgh District,
Corps of Engineers
Federal Building
1000 Liberty Avenue
Pittsburgh, PA 15222
(412) 644-4204

District Engineer
Huntington District,
Corps of Engineers
New Federal Building
502 Eighth Street
Huntington, WV 25701-2070
(304) 529-5487

District Engineer
Norfolk District,
Corps of Engineers
Fort Norfolk,
803 Front Street
Norfolk, VA 23510
(804) 441-3652

District Engineer
Wilmington District,
Corps of Engineers
P.O. Box 1890
Wilmington, NC 28401
(919) 343-4629

District Engineer
Buffalo District,
Corps of Engineers
1776 Niagara Street
Buffalo, NY 14207
(716) 876-5454

STATE

Delaware Department of Natural Resources and Environmental Control
Division of Wetlands and Underwater Lands
P.O. Box 1401
Dover, DE 19903
(302) 736-4691

Maryland Department of Natural Resources
Water Resources Administration
Tawes State Office Building
Annapolis, MD 21401
(301) 269-3871

Pennsylvania Department of Environmental Resources
Bureau of Dams and Waterways Management
P.O. Box 2357
Harrisburg, PA 17101
(717) 787-6827

Virginia Marine Resources Commission
P.O. Box 756
Newport News, VA 23607
(804) 247-2200

TAKE PRIDE IN AMERICA
HELP PROTECT OUR
NATION'S WETLANDS

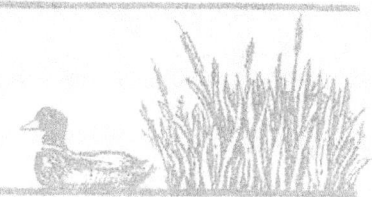

Elise Smith